Cute and Cuddly: Baby Animals

DUCKLINGS

By Katie Kawa

Gareth Stevens
Publishing

Please visit our website, www.garethstevens.com. For a free color catalog of all our high-quality books, call toll free 1-800-542-2595 or fax 1-877-542-2596.

Library of Congress Cataloging-in-Publication Data

Kawa, Katie.
Ducklings / Katie Kawa.
     p. cm. — (Cute and cuddly—baby animals)
ISBN 978-1-4339-5540-2 (pbk.)
ISBN 978-1-4339-5541-9 (6-pack)
ISBN 978-1-4339-5538-9 (library binding)
1. Ducklings—Juvenile literature. I. Title.
QL696.A52K376 2012
598.4'1139—dc22
                                        2011002136

First Edition

Published in 2012 by
Gareth Stevens Publishing
111 East 14th Street, Suite 349
New York, NY 10003

Copyright © 2012 Gareth Stevens Publishing

Editor: Katie Kawa
Designer: Andrea Davison-Bartolotta

Photo credits: Cover, pp. 1, 7, 9, 11, 13, 17, 24 (beak) Shutterstock.com; p. 5 Junko Kimura/Getty Images; pp. 15, 24 (feet) John Daniels/Dorling Kindersley/Getty Images; pp. 19, 24 (feathers) Hemera/Thinkstock; p. 21 iStockphoto.com; p. 23 Jupiterimages/liquidlibrary/Thinkstock.

Printed in the United States of America

CPSIA compliance information: Batch #CS11GS: For further information contact Gareth Stevens, New York, New York at 1-800-542-2595.

Contents

Ducklings are baby ducks.

5

A duckling comes from an egg. Its beak opens the egg.

7

Ducklings have soft feathers. These are called down.

A duckling needs to stay warm. Its feathers keep it warm.

Ducklings eat bugs, snails, and worms.

Ducklings have big feet.
This helps them swim.

Ducklings swim in cold water. Their feet cannot feel the cold.

Ducklings grow new feathers. They do not get wet!

19

Soon, ducklings can fly.

People keep ducklings as pets.

Words to Know

beak

feathers

feet

Index

24